A VISIT TO
India
REVISED AND UPDATED

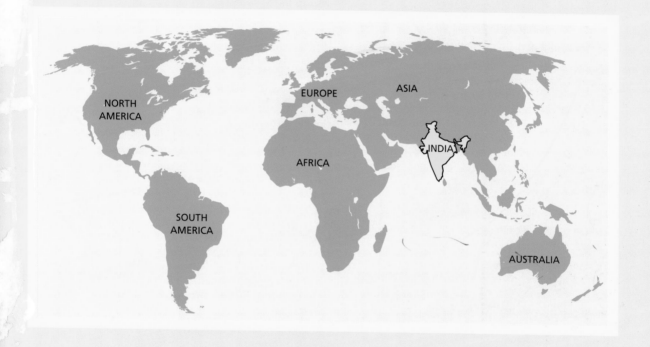

NORTH
AMERICA

EUROPE

ASIA

AFRICA

INDIA

SOUTH
AMERICA

AUSTRALIA

Peter and Connie Roop

Heinemann
LIBRARY

www.heinemann.co.uk/library

Visit our website to find out more information about Heinemann Library books.

To order:
☎ Phone 44 (0) 1865 888066
🖶 Send a fax to 44 (0) 1865 314091
💻 Visit the Heinemann Bookshop at www.heinemann.co.uk/library to browse our catalogue and order online.

Editorial: Sarah Shannon
Design: Joanna Hinton-Malivoire
Picture research: Mica Brancic
Production: Duncan Gilbert

Originated by Modern Age
Printed and bound in China by South China Printing Co. Ltd

ISBN 978 0 431087283 (hardback)
12 11 10 09 08
10 9 8 7 6 5 4 3 2 1

ISBN 978 0 431087429 (paperback)
12 11 10 09 08
10 9 8 7 6 5 4 3 2 1

British Library Cataloguing in Publication Data

Roop, Peter
A visit to India. - New ed.
1. India – Social conditions – 1947 –   – Juvenile literature
2. India – Geography – Juvenile literature
3. India – Social life and customs – 21st century – Juvenile literature
I.Title II.Roop, Connie III. India
954'.0532

Acknowledgements

The publishers would like to thank the following for permission to reproduce photographs: ©Alamy p. **22** (Jon Arnold Images Ltd/Walter Bibikow); ©Getty Images p. **13** (The Image Bank/Thomas Holton), p. **14** (Taxi/Dream Pictures); ©Hutchison Library pp. **10**, **23** (J Horner), p. **25** (J Highet); ©Images of India p. **27**; ©J Allan Cash Ltd pp. **7**, **8**, **15**, **18**, **21**, **28**, **29**; ©Magnum pp. **19**, **24** (R Raghu); ©Panos Pictures p. **6** (S Anwar), p. **5** (R Berriedale-Johnson), p. **16** (J Horner), p. **11** (Z Nelson), p. **20** (D O'Leary), pp. **9**, **26** (P Smith). ©Photolibrary p. **12** (Fresh Food Images/Hilary Moore); ©Reuters p. **17** (Sherwin Crasto).

Cover photograph of family walking through pavillion at Amber Palace. Jaipur, Rajasthan reproduced with permission of Lonley Planet Images (Richard I'Anson).

Our thanks to Nick Lapthorn and Clare Lewis for their help in the preparation of this book.

Every effort has been made to contact copyright holders of any material reproduced in this book. Any omissions will be rectified in subsequent printings if notice is given to the publishers.

Contents

Any words appearing in bold, **like this**, are explained in the Glossary.

India

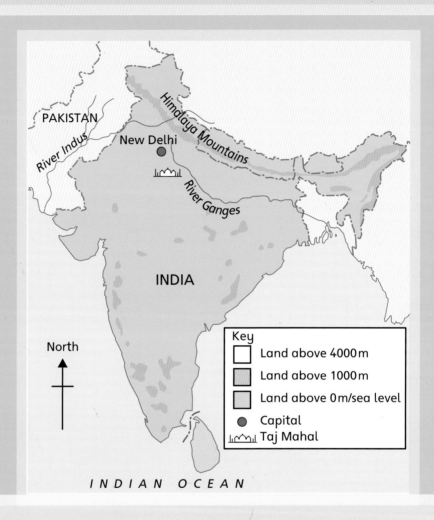

PAKISTAN

River Indus

New Delhi

Himalaya Mountains

River Ganges

INDIA

North

Key

Land above 4000 m

Land above 1000 m

Land above 0 m/sea level

● Capital

Taj Mahal

INDIAN OCEAN

India takes its name from the River Indus. This river runs through Pakistan, which used to be part of India. India is in Asia.

Many people live in India. Only China has more people than India. Most Indians live in the country, but the cities are very crowded.

Lots of people gather together for festivals or at the market.

India has three main types of land. In the north of the country are the Himalaya Mountains. These are the highest mountains in the world.

The middle of India forms one of the largest **plains** in the world. The other part of India is the **peninsula**. It has high, flat mountains and many kilometres of beautiful seashore.

Palm trees often grow along the sandy shoreline.

The Taj Mahal is India's most famous building. It was built over 300 years ago in memory of a much loved queen, called Mumtaz Mahal.

The River Ganges is over 2000 kilometres long.

The River Ganges is a long, wide river. To many Indians it is a holy river. There are many places along its banks where people pray and wash in it.

In the cities people live in small flats.
Many poor people live in huts or tents,
or have no homes at all. It is very
dangerous for these people during the
monsoon season.

Most people live in country villages. Some homes are made of **bamboo** or home-made clay bricks.

Large families often live together in one building.

Food

Many Indians eat only vegetables and seafood, cooked with fresh **spices**. Rice or bread is served with every meal. Indian breads are round and flat.

Lots of different spices are used in Indian food.

A very popular dish is tandoori, which is meat cooked in a very hot, clay oven. Another favourite meal is dhal, a thick **lentil** soup eaten with bread.

Clothes

Most Indian women wear **saris**. They are cool and comfortable. They can be very plain for work, or **embroidered** in beautiful colours for special days.

Some men wear loose trousers called pyjamas. Farmers wear dhotis, which are cloths tied round their waist. In the cities many people wear western clothes.

Work

Most Indians are farmers. They grow rice, tea, sugar cane, wheat, fruit and vegetables. The hot, wet weather is very good for growing **crops**.

Call centres are places where people answer telephone calls for companies.

Some people work in **factories** and make things such as cloth, computers, and cars. Many people now work in the **service industry** for western companies.

Transport

In the crowded streets you will see lorries, cars, scooters, bicycles, bicycle rickshaws (three-wheeled bicycles for passengers or heavy loads) and people on foot.

Most trains and buses are so full that people ride on the roof.

India's rivers are also very busy. Large and small boats carry people and **cargo** along them.

Languages

There are many different groups of people in India. Each group has its own **customs** and beliefs. Over 75 languages are spoken in India.

School is a good place to learn new languages.

Hindi is the most important language in India. Hindi and English are taught in schools so that Indians can speak to each other whatever their language.

School

Children go to school from the age of 6 to 14. They study lots of subjects, such as Hindi, English, maths, history and geography.

Some children have to work all day in the fields.

Many children are too poor to go to school. Their families need them to stay at home and help farm or beg in the streets.

Cricket is a popular sport in India. Children practise on the streets with a bat and ball. People also like to play hockey, badminton, polo and football (soccer).

One of the favourite entertainments in India is going to the cinema. Indian film stars are treated like heroes.

Families also enjoy funfairs in the early evening.

Celebrations

The different **religions** in India each have many festivals. Diwali is the Hindu New Year. It lasts for five days. Many lamps and fireworks make it a festival of light.

During the Pongal festival, cows are painted and decorated with flowers.

Hindus also believe that cows are holy. The festival of Pongal honours them.

The Arts

Many Indians enjoy making beautiful things from metal, wood, stone or cloth. Their paintings and clothes use bright colours and detailed patterns.

This man is making a beautiful dish.

The sitar is a famous Indian instrument.
It is like a guitar with up to 26 strings.
Sometimes its music is used for dancing
to. These dances often tell old stories.

Factfile

Name   The full name of India is the Republic of India.

Capital   The **capital** of India is New Delhi.

Language Most Indians speak Hindi and some English, but there are 75 other main types of language spoken in India.

Population There are over 1.1 billion people living in India.

Money   Instead of the dollar or pound, the Indians have the rupee.

Religions Most Indians believe in Hinduism (which worships many gods). As well as Hindus there are also some Muslims, Christians and Sikhs.

Products India produces lots of rice, wheat, tea, sugar, coffee, jewellery, clothes and machinery.

Words you can learn

do (daw)	two
tin (dean)	three
namaste (nahm-as-teh)	hello
namaste	goodbye
shukrinya	thank you
mehabani seh (meha-bani-seh)	please

Glossary

bamboo a tall plant with a long, strong stem

capital the city where the government is based

cargo things that are transported

crops the plants that are grown and harvested

customs the way people do things

embroidered stitches used to decorate material

factories places where many of the same things are made

lentil a kind of bean

monsoon season a time of very rainy weather

peninsula land with water on three sides

plain an area of open, flat land

religions what people believe in

saris long pieces of cloth wrapped around the waist and shoulders

service industry businesses that do things for people rather than making things

spices powder or seeds used to give food a strong, hot taste

Index